Soul Survivor
By
C. R. Clemens

"Soul Survivor," by C.R. Clemens. ISBN 1-58939-889-0.

Library of Congress Control Number: 2006928042

Internal graphics by Robert Ballard.

Published 2006 by Virtualbookworm.com Publishing Inc., P.O. Box 9949, College Station, TX 77842, US. ©2006, C.R. Clemens. All rights reserved. No part of this publication may be reproduced, stored in a retrieval system, or transmitted in any form or by any means, electronic, mechanical, recording or otherwise, without the prior written permission of C.R. Clemens.

Manufactured in the United States of America.

To my husband, Ralph, who believed in me and remained strong while the demons kept knocking on our door.

****

To Kelsey, Natalie, Colton, Austin, Kaylee, Easton, Polly and Tommy.
Keep your eyes on the heavenly angels.

"No, dear brothers, I am still not all I should be but I am bringing all my energies to bear on this one thing: Forgetting the past and looking forward to what lies ahead..." Philippians 3:13

Table of Contents

Preface i
The Real Deal 1
Hide N' Seek 12
Opening the Door 22
Dabbling 30
   Numerology **32**
   Palmistry **34**
   Psychometry **36**
   Crystals **40**
   Cards **44**
   Dreams & Visions **48**
   Ouija Board **54**
Which Spirit's Which? 62

Preface

My parents gave me a solid spiritual foundation. It was built on Sunday worship and twelve years of parochial school. Ever since I can remember, having faith in God and accepting Jesus Christ as our personal Savior have been the fundamental beliefs within our family. Yet, I somehow managed to drift into psychic phenomenon.

I am sure that you have noticed how easily small children can be enticed to disobey their parents once they have been turned loose in an environment filled with other children their own age. Many children will hold steadfast to what they have been taught at home. Still, there is always that one child that caves into the pressures surrounding him. As we grow up and enter the world as a young adult, many of the pressures that we experienced in high school still remain. Choices concerning alcohol, sex, crime and even the occult only intensify. While our minds are preoccupied by the novelty of being out from under the supervision of our parents, it is easy to push aside the spiritual guidance that they tried so hard to instill in us. Satan knows this and uses our human condition to his advantage.

Many authors have gone to great lengths to enlighten us on the spirits that roam this Earth and my book is not meant to contradict their teachings in any way. The purpose of my manuscript is to give you an inside view of the spiritual world as I experienced it over a course of twenty five years as well as proclaim the glory of God after witnessing His forgiving love. The stories are very real even though I have respectfully changed the names of the actual people who were involved in them. The scriptures that I have quoted have been taken from *The Book,* published by Tyndale House Publishers, Inc. This particular version was printed in 1984. I chose this version of the Bible because it is simple to read as well as understand.

God Bless

The Real Deal

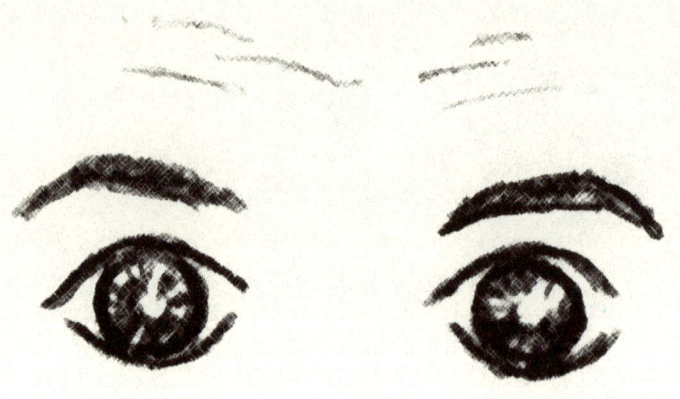

– 1 –

People often say that psychics are no more than swindlers making a living off of others who are vulnerable. I will not dispute the fact that some spiritualists are bogus. Nonetheless, even the Bible tells us that psychics do exist.

> *One day, as we were going down to the place of prayer beside the river, we met a demon-possessed slave girl, who was a fortune teller, and earned much money for her masters. (Acts 16:16)*

Throughout the twenty five years that I spent flirting with the supernatural, I developed a profound sense in this area that enabled me to distinguish the difference between a true psychic and a scam artist. I simply watched their eyes for the slightest change in color and listened to the resonance in their voice when I would challenge them about the truthfulness of their predictions. Those who were enlightened by the Spirit of Divination would have a dark cloudiness come over their pupils and I could hear a rich anger in their tone. I assure you, there are individuals in this world who do speak to us through this familiar spirit.

Could you spot these folks on the street? It is very unlikely. Contrary to what so many people believe about a psychic's wardrobe, it is very much the same as yours or mine. There are those that prefer to dress in unusual clothing. But, for the most part, you would not recognize them if they were shopping along side you at the grocery store. Maybe that man dressed in a suit and tie standing behind you in the check-out lane is reading the aura above your head. You could have a psychic sitting right next to you in the work place. Have you ever considered the possibility that your secretary might have extrasensory ability? Perhaps that stylish hair cut and those trendy new boots have not allowed you to think of her as anything more than a woman with good fashion sense. Still, there is the possibility that she is aware of much more than your business appointments for the day. Even though most psychics choose to do readings, séances or past life regression for their sole income, there are those who work regular eight to five jobs. They practice their special gift after hours.

It has been my observation that these atypical people live a very simple life style. Ninety eight percent of the psychics who have done readings for me were located in an apartment complex or a modest home in a family-oriented neighborhood. Perhaps you have one living right next door to you. I do not say this to alarm you; it is just a very common fact. I remember feeling anxious every time I went to visit a new psychic. I enjoyed experiencing the ambiance of their home almost as much as the tool they would use to do my reading. I have had my fortune told in a living room that was pitch black except for a desk lamp. A tape recorder was all that sat on the tattered card table where the psychic laid out her deck of fifty-two. On another occasion, I sat in a wicker chair and was offered a glass of ice tea and something to nibble on while the clairvoyant gazed over her crystal ball. I can only recall one time that I went to an actual business office. The atmosphere within those four walls was extremely cold and barren.

Reputable psychics prefer to blend in so that they do not draw attention to themselves. This comes from the belief that their knowledge is given to them by God. They are meant to help and heal others without being showy about it.

Take care! Don't do your good deeds publicly to be admired, for then you will lose the reward from your Father in Heaven. (Matthew 6:1)

Spiritualists take their job very seriously. The majority of them are not interested in advertising. The psychics I interviewed for the purpose of this book agreed that their clients are sent to them by God. However, they do accept new patrons on a referral basis. Although some of them do participate in Psychic Fairs

3

every now and then, most of them are only trying to make themselves more available to their clientele. A few of them confessed that they also enjoy fraternizing with the other psychics.

The spiritualists that I have known were usually in their late thirties or older. The consensus seems to be that the younger generation is not very eager to cultivate their talent nor make their abilities known to the public. I was unable to speak with any of the children who had been raised by these psychics. One or two of my subjects did reveal to me that their offspring had the same gift with which they themselves had been born. It appeared to be a cycle of some sort. Most of the psychics I spoke with explained to me that they had been reared by someone who also had a special gift.

After visiting with so many of these folks, I drew the conclusion that most psychics are divorced. I did not delve into their privacy and ask why because I have been divorced myself. I had to respect their right to their own personal lives. I am sure that these psychics have endured the same sorrow and pain as anyone else that has ever been through this type of experience.

> *Dear brothers, don't be too eager to tell others their faults, for we all make many mistakes... (James 3:1)*

One more piece of information that I found to be consistent throughout all the interviews that I conducted was that most spiritualists are female. The explanation that I was given for this was that women tend to be more intuitive than men. This is not to say that male psychics are not just as gifted, but that women are more prevalent in this arena.

When I inquired as to the authenticity of a "1-800" psychic, I got an overwhelming response... FRAUD! The psychics I spoke with feel that these fortune tellers give them a bad name. I was told that, once you are connected to one of these numbers, you are offered a package that allows you so many minutes to speak with the alleged spiritualist or you may be given a set number of questions you may ask them once they are actually on the line. The average client is easily convinced to purchase one of these packages. Before these victims realize it, they are spending hard-earned money to speak with someone who *claims* to be a genuine psychic. By the end of the reading, they are so amazed at the *insight* the so-called psychic has shown about their personal situation, that it is easy for them to call again when something else has frightened or confused them. I have never personally called one of these numbers. Therefore, this information is strictly second hand.

Another avenue into the psychic world is often lit up by neon signs as you are driving past your local strip mall. I have never allowed myself to drop into one of these establishments either. In spite of this, it is my understanding that you should enter these places at your own risk. A few of the psychics that I spoke with compared these people to charlatans that you might encounter in a public place. They are experts in body language and approach you in a comforting manner in an attempt to gain your confidence. This type of set up is where you are more than likely going to find a con artist who has been trained to take your money.

I have to admit that I was leery while making the decision to personally interview a number of psychics. I was afraid that I might be tempted by the curious nature that controlled my spirit in previous years and cheat on God once more. After giving it considerable thought, I knew that God would protect me from the snare of Satan. After all, the will of God was the reason that I needed to get insight directly from these people.

Dear children, keep away from anything that might take God's place in your hearts. Amen. (1John 5:21)

Yes! My past still haunts me from time to time. There are moments when an old prediction flits through my mind and I have to remind myself that some psychics *are* able to see the future, but their knowledge is not from God. It is at these times that I ask God to forgive me all over again and remove these memories from my psyche.

The survey that a number of psychics answered for me was very basic. I did not want to extort them as individuals. Aside from their marital status and age, the rest of my questions pertained to their personal gifts and spiritual convictions. As it turned out, I thoroughly enjoyed talking with the psychics who allowed me to interview them. I was upfront with them about the context of my book and they could not have been more warm and friendly. It seemed that each one with whom I spoke encouraged me to follow my aspiration with great enthusiasm. Our conversations were similar to those that I had with my psychic friends so many years ago. We laughed as we shared our views on different issues. Most of them offered to do a reading for me. They were very understanding when I graciously declined. Yet, a few of them felt the need to tell me *something* before our time was up.

During the course of one particular interview, I had mentioned that in the last visit that I had made to my favorite psychic, Jackie, it was revealed to me that one day I would be compelled by the Higher Powers to write a book. She said that it would be imperative for me to do so. This information struck a nerve with the clairvoyant to whom I was speaking. As I stood and turned towards the door at the end of the interview, she confirmed that this book was exactly what Jackie was talking about and that it would be quite successful. I looked back at her with a simple smile. I told her that I could see where this would be very possible since God wanted it to be written.

While driving home, I could not help but wonder what this psychic would have said about the rest of the prediction that Jackie had made pertaining to my book. You see, I had also been told that the core of my book would be in regards to some form of terrorism about which I was extremely knowledgeable. I was not into politics or third world countries back then. Therefore, I was completely oblivious as to what I had just heard. Today, as I observe our society, the pieces all seem to fit. People need a quick resolve in all aspects of their lives. The mystical realm offers them exactly that. How can I compare a psychic reading to terrorism? Well, the dictionary defines terrorism as a means of coercion. Once someone begins to open up their mind to a spiritualist, they also begin to repress their relationship with the Holy Spirit. A person cannot entertain an evil spirit and the spirit of God at the same time. Ultimately, Satan has achieved his goal which is to conquer a soul by turning it away from the truth of God's word and confusing it with his own lies.

Another psychic with whom I chatted informed me that I had begun my book at the right time. The Mercury Retrograde had not come into play yet. For those of you who are unfamiliar with this term, I will attempt to define it according to the teachings of astronomers. Each year all of the planets except for the Sun and the Moon have three or four retrograde periods. This means, that when viewed from the Earth, a planet will stop moving forward and begin to move backwards. This usually lasts approximately twenty one days. Psychics will tell you to remain flexible and to have a back up plan while the planet is in backward motion. Once the planet begins to move in a direct path again, those actions that are associated with it are safe to carry out.

I have always been told by psychics that Mercury is noted for ruling types of communication. This would include speaking to people and signing contracts or other papers of importance. They do not recommend performing these actions during this cycle. I was actually cautioned by one spiritualist to delay my vacation plans by one week because this period also has an effect on computerized machinery. She felt that I might incur flight cancellations or possibly have car trouble on the way to the airport. Her theory also embraced the idea that if someone has already started writing a proposal or begun to travel, they should have no problems due to the retrograde period. However, she mentioned that a person should be sure not to start anything brand new until the cycle has ended. I was unable to locate any information in the Bible on this subject, but there was one verse that caught my eye.

> Then he said, "Don't be frightened, Daniel, for your request has been heard in heaven and was answered the very first day you began to fast before the Lord and pray for understanding; that very day I was sent here to meet you. But for **twenty-one days** the mighty **Evil Spirit** who overrules the kingdom of Persia **blocked my way.**" (Daniel 10: 12, 13)

This is exactly what used to happen to me when I would ask God for His intervention. I would turn right around and visit with a psychic while I was waiting on Him to make His move. Yet, how could He? I had placed an evil force directly in His path. As to the notion that there are certain times of the year that we should not start something new in our lives, God's word does not mention the planets retrograde period.

> *Ask, and you will be given what you ask for. Seek, and you will find. Knock and the door will be opened.... (Matthew 7:7)*

By the time I had concluded all of my interviews with various psychics, a part of me had grown weary. I was amazed at the many different gifts that they all practiced. Reading tarot cards, gazing over a crystal ball and speaking through a trance were just a few of the gifts about which I was instructed. A handful of these folks struck me as being sincere in their belief that the spirit of God was working through them. Still, others touched my heart with a darkness that I cannot put into words. Upon returning home after each appointment, I took a moment to pray for them and ask God to protect the lost people who seek them out.

> *Then the fifth angel poured out his flask upon the throne of the Creature from the sea, and his kingdom was plunged into darkness. And his subjects gnawed their tongues in anguish, and*

cursed the God of Heaven for their pains and sores, but they refused to repent of all their evil deeds. (Revelations 16:10,11)

Hide N' Seek

-2-

The people with whom I have spoken about my history of visiting psychics always wanted to know if I really believed in this supernatural phenomenon. The only way to answer their question was to clarify that I believed in the capability that certain people possessed to know things. I still do!

It was during the seventies era when I began stumbling into Satan's web of deception. I never doubted that God was the ultimate force in my life. Still, I was young and searching for something tangible to hold onto whenever I became frightened or confused. This decade did not just offer love beads and the peace sign. Horoscopes, dream books and other psychic phenomenon were highly accepted during this period. I carried my dream dictionary with me everywhere I went. I also had a book that explained which signs of the zodiac were well-suited for a romantic relationship. I kept it on my bedside table. There were even cycles when I deliberated over a Ouija Board. Mix all of this together and you have the perfect recipe for a lost soul. But, wait! There was more to it than this.

As wonderful as it might have been to be pampered and protected during our childhood, for some of us it brought on a rebellious frame of mind once we were old enough for the apron strings to be cut. After years of being shown that we needed someone older and wiser to get through life, some of us were ready to prove our loved ones wrong. I could not wait to be out of my parent's house. I lacked the necessary skills such as cooking, budgeting and so forth. Nevertheless, I was determined to make it on my own. Independence was like a drug to me. I had gotten so high on it that I did not realize what I was doing half of the time. The receptionist job that I held down was an effortless task. My finances were holding their own. I had become a regular at a certain fraternity house due to my boyfriend who I had been dating for a couple of years. During the week, I played hard with the friends I had made at the office. In between all of this, I eked out some time to pursue my passion for the spirit world. All in all, I was living the life. Sweet freedom definitely had its perks.

> ... *For rebellion is as bad as the sin of witchcraft, and stubbornness is as bad as worshipping idols. (1Samuel 15:23)*

I was very secretive about my personal life when I was in contact with my family. Even though there was no doubt in my mind that they had a pretty good idea of what I was doing, coming right out and *saying* what I had been up to would have just given them an opening to lecture me. Still, the day finally came when I opened my mouth and inserted my foot about a reading I had just had done! You can imagine how perplexed my family was when they became aware that I was investigating the psychic world. Although they were concerned for me spiritually, I interpreted their disapproval as unnecessary criticism. At one point, I can remember telling my mother that it was comforting to be able to tell a psychic my thoughts and know that they would actually *listen* to me. Her rebuttal was based on the reality that I had gone from getting free advice from the people that truly cared about me to paying a stranger for guidance even though I meant nothing to them at all.

> *These teachers in their greed will tell you anything to get hold of your money. But God condemned them long ago and their destruction is on the way. (2 Peter 2:3)*

In my early twenties, I had begun to fall into a mild depression. The good times seemed to be fading away. One by one, my friends had started to rearrange their priorities in life and I still had not figured out what mine were. My boyfriend and I decided that we'd had a good run, but he was not ready to get married and I could not handle the idea of being alone the rest of my life. My finances were a mess because I had become a credit card junkie. I believe I carried seven of them on me for emergencies such as new jeans, gasoline and treating myself to a good restaurant every now and then. The personnel agency where I had been working was run by a man who was constantly sexually harassing me. There was no reason for me to take action against him because, in that day and age, you could not simply file a complaint and expect someone to believe you. The despair that I was feeling about my overall existence finally brought me to my knees. I asked God for direction, but He did not seem to be listening. So, I contacted a psychic. She told me that I would be receiving an invitation in the near future that would resolve my current situation. A few weeks later, I had a call from my girlfriend, Darlene. We had been best friends all through high school. She and Charlotte, her friend from college, were living in Houston and needed a third roommate. Score one for the psychic! It took me less than five minutes to agree to move south by mid summer.

I had my doubts about sharing an apartment with someone other than Darlene. Nevertheless, the three of us meshed well together. The first six months that I lived with them were incredibly fun! I took a job as a bank teller at the institution where Darlene was working. I thoroughly enjoyed meeting new people every day. The dread of ill will that I had brought along with me quickly faded. I was the new kid in town and everyone was glad to see me. Our apartment complex was the perfect place to hang out. There was always something going on around the pool and to my surprise a few of our neighbors were into psychic phenomenon! I will never forget how excited Charlotte was when Darlene told her that I had psychic ability! Although I had never considered her proclamation to be true, I understood why Darlene felt that way. She had been an eye witness to my uncanny talent a number of times over the years. From that moment on, Charlotte and I had found a mutual interest that would keep us up at night for months to come.

It was around a year later when my life steadily began to feel humdrum. My job had become second nature to me and my new friends were now just part of my routine. As a matter of fact, a lot of them had actually moved on to achieve their goals as young adults. I had grown weary of the rainy season and do not even get me started on the traffic! I was still having a rough time financially, too. Obviously, finances were not my strong suit. There were moments when I would find myself trying to remember why I had moved away from home in the first place. One night, while I was driving home from work, I burst into tears. When I arrived at our apartment, my roommates thought something horrible had happened to me. I explained to them that something *had* happened. I wanted to go home! I can remember phoning my parents and telling them that I could not get past the sadness that I was experiencing. I sobbed through the entire conversation. My dad questioned me as to

17

whether or not I had gotten into a bad situation or possibly had made a poor choice while I was out with my friends. When I promised him that I was not in any kind of trouble, he simply said, "Honey, why don't you just come home?" For the first time in my life, I accepted the fact that he was truly concerned for his daughter and not just criticizing my behavior.

Within six months, I was cruising down I-45 headed north. My folks were going to let me stay with them for a few months until I found a job and got back on my feet. I certainly was not thrilled about having to reside in their home again, but I was thankful that I had a temporary place to live. The independence that had once felt like freedom in my life had become like a yoke that was bearing down on my shoulders. There is nothing wrong with trying your wings in a new place. However, I had started to realize, that by moving away from my problems, I had possibly missed out on something far more noteworthy to do with my life. Was it possible that the psychic had been speaking about a different invitation that would have opened up new opportunities for me? Better still, what if I had stayed in my small apartment and waited for God to answer my prayers? I will never know for sure. The one thing I do believe is that my life would have turned out very differently if I had kept *my* will out of the picture and patiently allowed God to do *His* will through me.

Fortunately, my family never turned their back on me. Although we did not see eye to eye, when I made the decision to move away, I knew that I could always turn to them no matter how bad things might become. Sadly, the countless children in today's society, who have been scarred by abuse or divorce, are often cast out by those they need the most. Their age could be anywhere from seven to fifty. The psychological baggage they carry around grows heavier by the day. Most of them are looking for a place to store it. I can understand why some spiritualists have such a booming business. I used to think of them as my secret pals to whom I could unload all my troubles.

The clientele that walks in and out of a psychic's door includes people of all ages and all walks of life. The youngest of these is more than likely a college student or a person in their early twenties. They are just starting out in life and have a great need to receive approval as well as direction. Someone in their late twenties or early thirties would be next. Their life is usually beginning to unfold according to their dreams or accomplishments. Maybe they are contemplating a career move and need confirmation in reference to a job they have been offered. A person nearing the age of forty would succeed them. It would not be out of the question for an investment broker to seek counsel over a new client's good fortune. As adults approach that ever so popular uphill battle over turning fifty, there are numerous reasons why they might wander into a psychic's parlor. The need to be validated and reassured that their life is not really over can be unrelenting. Once the golden years arrive, it is fairly common for a senior citizen to have lost touch with loved ones over the years. They often seek out a spiritualist to see how the lives of their long lost friends have turned out.

I can be very honest about my past now, but I hid my involvement with psychics for many years. I told myself that it was not anyone's business how I spent my time or my money. If someone did find out, I shrugged it off as a way to have fun. I was actually concealing the guilt and the embarrassment that I felt. My faith had been rooted in God. Deep inside, I knew that I was going against Him. When people began finding out that I was writing this book, I was amazed at how many of them pulled me over to the side and whispered that they had been to a psychic in their younger days. I found it interesting that they still felt shame for something they had done so long ago. I responded by telling them that it took me a very long time to ask for God's forgiveness for my sin, but that I knew He had forgiven me. I suggested that they do the same. The very day that I permitted myself to forgive those who had emotionally bruised me in the past was the same day that I began to take a realistic look at my involvement with the mystical arena. Forgiveness is a strong weapon against the familiar spirits. Think of it as a repellent for your soul. Once you learn to forgive, God's light emerges and begins to penetrate the darkness where your pain and anger dwell.

If you speak with someone who has seen a spiritualist of any kind, ask them if they have ever experienced an event in their life that left them feeling totally inadequate in some way. I believe you will find that there was at least one incident in their past that they have never been able to forget. Normally, when we cannot put such an event behind us, we also cannot forgive those who were involved. If you find this to be true, take a few minutes out of your day and say a prayer for them.

Admit your faults to one another and pray for each other so that you may be healed... (James 5:16)

Opening the Door

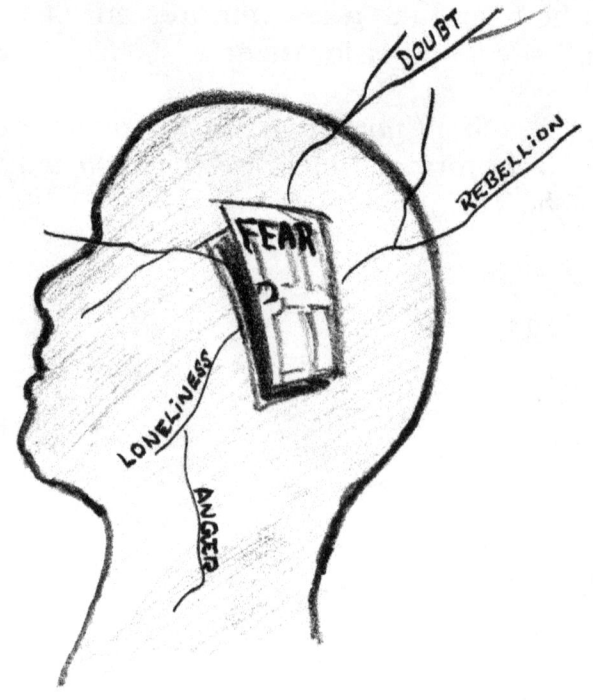

-3-

There will always be a time in our life when we are forced to choose between one thing or another. It might be as simple as continuing to make repairs on a vehicle that we have already paid off rather than trading it in for a brand new model. Then, again, there are more serious matters such as remaining in an abusive relationship instead of fleeing from danger and starting a new life. Whatever the circumstances, the Bible teaches us to trust in God.

> *He will keep in perfect peace all those who trust in him, whose thoughts turn often to the Lord! Trust in the Lord God always, for in the Lord Jehovah is your everlasting strength. (Isaiah 26:3,4)*

We are to remain in the Spirit of God and pray earnestly about every decision that we face. The hours that we spend worrying over our dilemmas do nothing more than drain us both in body and soul. When I am fearful about making a vital change in my life, I lean heavily on the fact that when God closes a door, He opens a window. In other words, whatever I must leave behind should be left without fretfulness. God always has something else waiting for me that has a much greater purpose in my life. We are put on this Earth to please God, not ourselves. In spite of this, we continuously put this certainty out of our minds.

When the answers to our prayers are not exactly what we want to hear, it is almost a reflex to act as though we have never heard them. Once we avoid the truth that the Holy Spirit has delivered to us, we have turned away from God. This in itself is a sin. Therefore, it is at this exact moment that we "open a door" to an evil spirit. He jumps in and makes himself right at home. From this point forward, this same spirit does everything he can to make sure that we sin over and over again. We continue to lie, remain jealous, harbor anger and so forth. I continued to fear the unknown and seek out knowledge from the Spirit of Divination.

There are other ways to "open a door" for Satan's soldiers. Did you know that the mind is the doorway to the soul? If we do not take preventative measures to guard against leaving it wide open for these demons to use as their personal playground, we are asking for trouble in our spiritual life.

> *So use every piece of God's armor to resist the enemy whenever he attacks, and when it is all over, you will be standing up... And you will need the*

helmet of salvation and the sword of the spirit—which is the Word of God. (Ephesians 6:13,17)

Sometimes, we are totally unaware that we have prepared an area for an evil spirit to set up shop within our minds. Do you know someone who has undergone hypnosis for overeating or perhaps to quit smoking? This is an opportunity that an evil spirit would take advantage of because the mind is in a passive state. It becomes an easy target. What type of music do you listen to? Have you ever participated in a group that promotes some type of motivational tapes? Both of these activities can have subliminal messages in them that are meant to convey demonic messages to the mind. How much thought do you put into choosing your children's toys? There are a few out there that can open a demonic door within the mind of an innocent child.

For instance, when I was a young child, my sister and I enjoyed spending the night at our aunt's house. She was so much fun! Inevitably, she would find something new and exciting to share with us each time that we would visit. One of these unforgettable sleepovers involved a game that was different from those that my sister and I played at home. The name of this game was Ouija Board! My aunt explained to us that, if you asked the board something you wanted to know, it would spell out the answer to your question. At that age, we did not fully understand how this was possible. Nonetheless, we trusted her without reservation and went ahead and played the game. My sister looked at this activity as just a silly way to pass the time. I was inquisitive as to how this board knew things. As I recall, my aunt referred to the board's source as a spirit. This quieted my curiosity about the game, but it brought up another concern. Ghosts! I went off to bed trying to picture what this ghost must have looked like as well as where it lived.

   I was entering the ninth grade before I saw a Ouija Board again. This time it was at a friend's house. She had invited several of us over to spend the night and celebrate the beginning of our freshman year. The board belonged to her parents, but she managed to sneak it into her bedroom before we all arrived. The girls were anxious to inquire about their boyfriends and other teenage concerns even though none of them had ever seen a Ouija Board prior to this party. You can imagine how quickly I became the center of attention when I remembered how to play with it. I was finally acknowledged by my peers for doing something exceptional in their eyes. After that night, I was the girl who knew things! When you are thirteen, you really do not care why your friends accept you. The bottom line is that they do.

   During the next four years, I became extremely fascinated by ghosts and life after death. Classmates constantly wanted to know why I had such weird interests. I could never explain to them why they looked at death in a perfectly normal way and I saw it as an adventure. I was totally ignorant to the fact that a familiar spirit was working inside of me. It must have crept in through the door that had been opened so many years before. I also developed a profound intuitive sense during my high school years. Still, it was not always easy having such an insightful spirit. I think we can all recall how important it was as a teenager to feel accepted by our peers.

Unfortunately, my reputation for having unusual foresight during my adolescence often left me feeling very isolated. Nonetheless, there were those who did manage to reap a few rewards by maintaining their friendships with me. I was never surprised when a note was passed along to me in the hallway at school asking me to concentrate on a specific relationship problem. It was also fairly common for someone to phone me in the evening about their significant other or the lack of one as the case may be. Although I did not believe that I really had psychic powers, I would attempt to find the answer to questions by concentrating as I fell asleep at night. It was strange how many mornings I would awake with a certain thought or idea that pertained to the dilemma that I had been discussing with someone the night before. By the time graduation arrived, I had been helpful in uniting and reuniting couples who went on to get married. What became of my intuitive spirit after I turned in my cap and gown? My "gift" as well as my involvement with the mystical realm reached much higher levels as I got older.

While I was raising my children, I hid my passion for the supernatural. We read the Bible and became involved in our church. I even taught some of the youth classes after a while. Unfortunately, as I drug them through the trials of divorce, they still overheard or were actually told about my secret. Whenever they would question me about my involvement with psychic phenomenon, I was truthful about my past activity in this area. I also discouraged them from taking the same route that I had chosen. I explained to them that my past spoke for itself. This made it easier for them to understand that I had suffered a great deal, both financially and spiritually, throughout my adult life because of my waywardness. I thank God everyday that my children have found their way by relying on their faith in Him rather than seeking out clairvoyants or a deck of tarot cards.

Familiar spirits lurk around our children from the moment that they are conceived. Throughout childhood, these same evil spirits are just waiting for the right moment to captivate a youngster's naive mind. As adolescence approaches, these same spirits are on hand to mentally escalate the struggles that teenagers face. Maybe this is the reason why so many young adults continue to carry a grudge over an event from their past.

I would suggest that you consider how all-embracing the mind of a young child is before you purchase a "Magic 8 Ball" or any other item for sale in the toy department that relates to magic or the supernatural. I would think twice about voting "yes" to having a fortune teller at the school carnival or senior prom. I urge you to consider the possibility that your own child may very well turn to a psychic one day. Why? Because everyone needs a confidential friend who will listen to their feelings and applaud their dreams once they become a young adult.

And now a word to you parents. Don't keep on scolding and nagging your children, making them angry and resentful. Rather, bring them up with the loving discipline the Lord Himself approves, with suggestions and godly advice. (Ephesians 6:4)

Dabbling

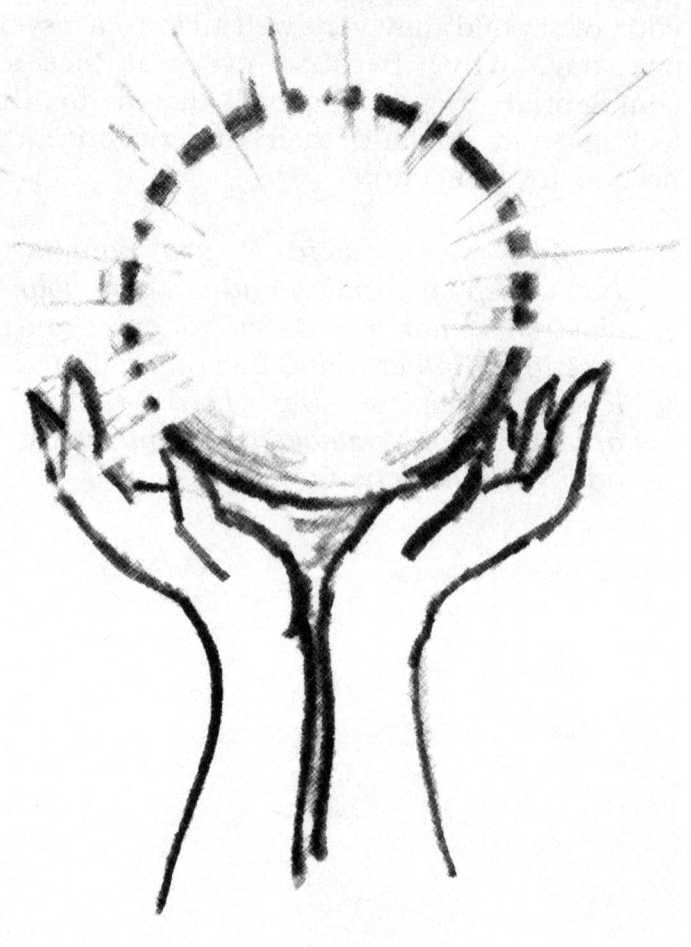

–4–

The tools that psychics use can be the most intriguing element within the mystical realm. I know it certainly was for me. I can still remember the rush that I would feel whenever I would have a reading done via a new tool. Looking back, I can see where these props were the true "hook" for me. I was comparable to a fisherman who needs to experience the use of a new lure. I could not wait to see what type of information might come from each one. In order to clarify how mesmerizing these articles can be, I am going to reveal the essence of the tools that I experienced. Please keep in mind that I was being drawn into this sphere by the familiar spirits and the following information is not meant to entice anyone to actually visit a psychic.

"So don't be anxious about tomorrow. God will take care of your tomorrow too. Live one day at a time." (Matthew 6:34)

Numerology

My first encounter with a psychic was in my early twenties. Linda, who was a counselor where I worked, recognized that I was having problems in my personal life and suggested that I visit a spiritualist. At first I thought she was joking. I knew that she was deep-rooted into astrology because we had discussed the idea of her charting my horoscope. Still, I had no idea that she was also into psychic readings. I expressed my concerns to her about tossing away my cash on someone who could be a fake. Linda swore to me that she knew a woman who had a reputation of being *right on the money* with any reading she had ever done. Since I was still feeling a bit of apprehension, I questioned Linda as to how much of my personal information this psychic would require if I made an appointment. I was told that she would only need my first name. This factor clenched the deal for me. I assumed that if all someone knew about me was my first name, then they could not possibly be a scam artist!

Within a week, I was sitting at a card table across from an elderly woman who reminded me a great deal of my grandmother. Her voice was soft and there was a sharpness in her eyes that gave me confidence in her ability to help me solve my problems. She started out by telling me things that I felt were very general. Her advice about my money problems was similar to something my parents had already told me. All I had to do was stop spending my paycheck foolishly and start saving some of it for a rainy day. When the subject of my troubled relationship came up, she told me that it was quite normal to experience break-ups at my age because most young men preferred to live a little rather than tie themselves down. I was losing interest fast when she suddenly looked into my eyes and began talking about a party that I was going to attend. She rattled off several of the names of those who would be there. When she explained that one young man would not be able to join us, my heart stood still! You see, I was putting together a class reunion that was to be held within the next few months. The names that she had spouted off were on my list. Furthermore, I had recently found out that one of our former classmates had died in a boating accident and I had not told *anyone* about his death. As I left her home that day, I was definitely convinced that I had been in the presence of a true psychic.

What I did not realize was that this woman had used numerology. The fact that she had me write down my birth date on a little piece of paper should have sent up a red flag in my mind. However, I was so engrossed in her performance that I did not even consider the actuality that I had just given her my age. It does not take a rocket scientist to figure out how many years it has been since someone has graduated from high school. Think about what young people enjoy most at this age. That's right, a party! Now, let's take a look at that invitation list. How many friends do you have that were given a name that was popular during the time you were conceived? Yep! I never even saw it coming. Still, how do you explain her knowledge of my deceased classmate?

I do not claim to know all of the ins and outs of numerology. In spite of this, I can tell you that numbers and the alphabet are involved. Each letter has a number assigned to it. How this tells a reader anything about a person is beyond my grasp. There *is* something that I am positive about. If someone can actually give you a prediction based on numbers, they undeniably must have the Spirit of Divination in their corner because this means of receiving knowledge has nothing at all to do with the Holy Spirit.

Palmistry

At one point in time, there was a famous psychic who read palms by mail. The interesting side to this story is that people in the work place were sending Xerox copies of their palms to her even though most of them denied having any belief in psychics. It seemed that everyone wanted to find out how long they were going to be single or if they would have a substantial income in the future. I certainly got in on the action because the cost for this reading was a meager fee. The crowd pleaser of this activity was that you did not even have to make an appointment! This reader could see your past and look at your present from a simple palm print she received in her private mail box. Even though there were those who said it was the easiest type of fortune telling to fake, the mail slots were constantly in use. I vividly remember watching my own mail box with intense curiosity. The day that I finally received my cassette tape that was packaged in a brown protective envelope, was the same day that I received confirmation that my first marriage was not working.

The first thing that I heard this woman's voice say was, "You are young at heart, but face a tremendous amount of responsibility." She continued to explain that my perseverance in my current situation would be short lived. My love line had revealed a relationship would be broken off. Wow! I was overwhelmed that she could know about my personal problems without ever meeting me. I automatically assumed that she was referring to the marital problems that I was having and the toll that they were taking on me. My husband was on workman's compensation and we had two children to take care of with another one on the way. I was holding down a high pressure job and trying to keep up with the kids as well as the bills. I had not considered a divorce at this point. However, after listening to this reading, I undoubtedly could see where it might become an alternative. She also stated that my prosperity line did not forecast a strong financial future. This made perfect sense to me when I thought about the financial burden that a single mother would face.

Have you ever heard of the power of suggestion? Well, due to the strong opinions I had about psychics at the time, I automatically took every word this woman had recorded and applied them to my real life situation. I was so desperate to find a quick fix to my weary existence that I gave up on waiting for the wisdom of the Holy Spirit. This is not to say that my marriage would have lasted a lifetime, but I certainly opened the door to the Spirit of Divination. Remember, the mind is the most likely place that an evil spirit will set up shop.

Psychometry

I had an experience several years ago that literally sent chills up my spine. I was going to visit my girlfriend, Lori, in Oklahoma City for the weekend. In the course of planning our time together, she had set up an appointment for both of us with a local psychic about whom she had heard. By the time I arrived Friday evening, something unexpected had come up and she had decided not to keep her appointment on Saturday. She offered me the keys to her car and directions to the psychic's home so that I could still go and check the woman out. I accepted even though I had wanted to experience this escapade with her at my side.

During my reading, this psychic insisted that my deceased grandmother was trying to tell me something. I was told a story that was totally unfamiliar to me. She was adamant about me acknowledging that the first letter of my grandmother's name was "B." I argued with her about this until she finally said it did not matter one way or the other. The emphasis was to be placed on the message itself. My dear old deceased grandmother wanted me to know that she was watching out for me. While laughing aloud, I told this psychic that I did not believe a word she was saying because the name she kept referring to was unfamiliar to me. I requested that she give me the cassette tape on which she had recorded my session and I left.

When I returned to Lori's house, she was anxious to hear all about my reaction to this psychic. I told her a few of the predictions that I had been given and then began explaining to her what had happened towards the end of my reading. Without any warning, Lori turned as pale as a ghost and was shaking terribly. As I walked over to her, she told me that the story that the psychic had told me was actually about the day that *her* grandfather had died. She could not believe that this woman had given such a detailed description of the actual events of that day. We decided to listen to the tape to verify the story, but that particular section of the recording was silent. We sat there on her bed for at least an hour trying to figure out what had just occurred.

As we retraced our steps from early that morning, an unnerving hunch came over both of us. The weather had taken a substantial dive in temperature and *I* had worn *Lori's* jacket to the reading! Could it have been possible that this woman had actually done a reading about my girlfriend instead of me? I made a quick phone call to the psychic. She confirmed that by wearing my friend's jacket it was *very likely* that she had merged our two separate energies. Needless to say, I truly believed that I had been in the home of a wicked individual. Although I had seen a crucifix on the wall and a statue of the Virgin Mary sitting on the coffee table, for the first time in all the years that I had played with different psychics I was frightened.

Your own wickedness will punish you. You will see what an evil, bitter thing it is to rebel against the Lord your God, fearlessly forsaking Him, says the Lord Almighty. (Jeremiah 2:19)

Although Hollywood treats this form of spiritualism as a novel idea, it has been around for decades. In the seventies, it was not uncommon for a police detective to turn to a well known psychic when they had reached a dead end in a missing person case. The family involved would provide an article of clothing or possibly a significant toy if a child was missing. It would be given to a medium so that they could touch the object and pick up on the energy of the owner. It was said that this energetic connection "broke down the barriers" that the police were facing. Hopefully, the authorities would be pointed in the right direction and they would be able to locate the victim.

I cannot help but shudder when I consider how much influence the Spirit of Divination will have on our children as they strive to become well adjusted adults. Most parents probably do not realize the spiritual destruction that can occur in the present day from allowing their children to watch certain television programs or some of the films being produced within the motion picture industry. Scriptwriters portray psychics to be noteworthy. Repeatedly, a spiritualist identifies the bad guy or gets to the bottom of a victim's death by using their ability to communicate with the dead. Have you ever seen a notation at the beginning of one of these programs that reads "parental discretion advised"? The biggest red flag for me is when these spiritualists never get any sleep. They are constantly disturbed by nightmares or the walking dead. Is this the way God intended for us to find peace? I find it disturbing that we are told by the media to monitor video games that our children play as well as the websites or chat rooms they enter into on the Internet, yet nothing is said about protecting our children spiritually by refusing to endorse psychic phenomenon as a means of entertainment. I consider this way of thinking to rank right up there with not allowing God in our schools. The influence of the familiar spirits *is* working within our society. Look around you and take note of the violent behavior patterns of children that are reported every day on the news. It certainly is not the Holy Spirit encouraging them to take weapons to school or perform occult rituals on one another.

    I personally do not believe that we are to make an attempt to disturb the spirits of the departed. According to scripture, when we die we leave *everything* behind. This includes our knowledge, our hopes and the chance to repent for whatever sins we have on our souls when we leave this world.

> *For the living at least know that they will die! But the dead know nothing; they don't even have their memories. Whatever they did in their lifetimes— loving, hating, envying—is long gone, and they have no part in anything here on earth anymore (Ecclesiastes 9:5,6)*

Crystals

As a child, I was always intrigued by werewolf movies. It was not the anguished man turning into a furry killer that captivated me, but the old gypsy woman that would gaze into her crystal ball just before the moon would come up. My imagination would escalate every time I saw her do this. I can remember closing my eyes and pretending that I could see what she saw in her crystal ball. This fantasy faded once I started to outgrow this type of amusement. When I was approaching my late twenties, I was invited to attend a Psychic Fair at a nearby hotel. It did not take long before my adolescent imagination came alive again.

The moment I walked through the door of the hotel ballroom, I knew that I was born to explore the mystical side of life! There was something for anyone who wanted knowledge about their inner spirit. Merchants were set up in the middle of this spacious room. Some were selling potions and lotions while others promoted herbal remedies. In addition to these, you could purchase more expensive items such as jewelry and crystals.

I was drawn to the stones. They were so beautiful and the woman selling them was quite informative. I was told that you could wear one around your neck and keep your inner-self centered. It has been said that a crystal puts out an electric energy like that of a quartz watch. I was fascinated to learn that different crystals carry a different type of energy. While I was speaking to the vendor about a particular crystal that had caught my eye, I noticed a shaft of light that kept flashing on the ceiling. As I turned around to see what might be causing this, I found myself staring at a magnificent crystal ball! Inexplicably, the stone I had been interested in was left behind as I instantly walked over to the booth where this gorgeous ball was sitting. I could have stood there the entire day looking at the array of crystal balls that were for sale. The stands that they had been placed upon were almost as enticing as the balls themselves. I searched to find something I could afford to take home with me. The lowest price I found was still too rich for my blood. I made a promise to myself that someday I would have one of those remarkable toys.

That day came about fifteen years later. I was in a marriage that was terminal. My spouse had reached a point in his dependency where his undying hope to remain married to me had led him to trying to buy my love. At Christmas, he surprised me with a beautiful crystal ball that sat on top of elephants harnessed by their trunks and tails. I was speechless! Not only had he *found* a crystal ball, but he had also located my favorite things to collect...elephants with their trunks up! I did not even stop to realize how wrong it was for me to accept his gift. I was already running for the phone to call Jackie. She had offered to teach me how to read a mystical ball a few months earlier.

> *"Burn their idols and do not touch the silver or gold they are made of. Do not take it or it will be a snare to you, for it is horrible to the Lord your God. Do not bring an idol into your home and worship it, for then your doom is sealed. Utterly detest it, for it is a cursed thing." (Deuteronomy 7:25,26)*

Within the week, I had received my tutorial on owning a crystal ball. Jackie gave me clear instructions on how to cleanse it of any evil spirits that might be attached to it and also how to prepare the ball for gazing. If you had the gift of vision, seeing into it would happen naturally. She definitely felt that I did have this gift and had expressed this to me several times in the past.

I had made a spot for my crystal ball on the chest of drawers in our bedroom. Still, I was not as eager as I had thought I would be to actually see something in this ball of glass. Something was cautioning me deep inside to disregard this gift of guilt. Nonetheless, my curiosity got the best of me and I started to look into it for a few seconds at a time. A few weeks passed by and I had yet to notice any images trying to come through. I began to relax about having this psychic tool in my home because it was obvious that I did not have any supernatural power after all.

It was just two days later when I *saw myself* in the crystal ball. I was dressed in an outfit that I had given away almost a year earlier. I was not crazy... I was not seeing things... it was me! Finally, my fantasy had come true. Over the next few days, I could not help but check for visualization over and over again. However, I never saw anything after that one time. That is, I did not see any *images*.

The truth of the matter is that I became quite frightened of my treasured crystal ball. One morning, as I was passing by it on my way out of the bedroom, I stopped dead in my tracks. I noticed the colors in the ball were swirling around and continuously getting darker. There was not a rational explanation for this phenomenon. All of a sudden, I felt a chill sway past me! All I could think of was how badly I wanted out of the house. I rushed off to work as I promised God that I would destroy that cursed plaything as soon as I came home that night. It was not easy; but, I did it. That gesture was the first real step I took in actually walking away from the mystical world.

Cards

Owning a crystal ball was not the only thing that I promised myself at that psychic fair. While I was wandering around the massive ballroom, watching all sorts of readings being done, I noticed a girl who appeared to be extremely agitated with a particular psychic named Iris. I asked a lady standing next to me what was going on. The woman turned to face the main entrance and pointed at a huge chalkboard on the wall. The name of every psychic in the fair was on it. My new acquaintance went on to enlighten me about the fifteen minute time slots where people could sign up to visit with the psychic of their choice. Apparently, this near hysterical girl had driven a long distance just to have her reading done by Iris. To her dismay, all of the psychic's slots were filled. I was instantly intrigued. I walked over to the table where Iris was sitting and realized that she was using a deck of fifty two instead of tarot cards to do her readings. I took this as a *sign* that I must have a reading by this psychic! You see, the phrase "read 'em and weep" sums up a great deal of my life. I have always loved to play card games of any kind. The way that all of this was falling together could only mean one thing... I *would* be read by Iris! As it turned out, I had several readings done by this psychic over a period of the following two and a half years. On occasion, I even referred a few of my friends to her.

However, the last time I saw her, something hardened my heart to Iris.

Towards the end of my relationship with this psychic, I met Julie who was the sister of one of my co-workers. She and I had become very close, very quickly. One weekend, while she was staying at my apartment, a severe ice storm hit. We ended up stranded within the complex for almost seventy two hours together. It was during this time that the two of us found out that we had more in common than we had thought. After playing backgammon for two days straight, Julie suggested that we play cards instead. Naturally, this did not bother me a bit. You should have seen my face when she whipped out her very own deck of fifty-two and began laying them out in a pattern that was totally familiar to me! The only thought that went through my head was that I had to learn how to do this. Julie was willing to teach me the meaning of the individual cards, but conveyed the fact that her cards were truly *hers* and that I would not be able to read them. I had never been told that, in order to read cards, you had to *season* them. This means that you have to do something with them that allows them to absorb your personal energy. Julie decided that she would allow me to try to season her cards by sleeping with them under my pillow for a few nights. We were both thrilled the next time we got together. I was able to lay the deck of cards out and get a message from them. Of course, I had to use a cheat sheet that Julie had provided for me, but still...

About a month later, Julie wanted to be read by a professional psychic. I sent her to see Iris with a grand recommendation. Once the reading was over, Julie called me wanting to know why I had ever gone to this woman in the first place. I was shocked! It seemed that Iris had been overly rude to my friend and told her not to come back. Just to be fair, I made an appointment with Iris to find out her side of the story. When I arrived, her apartment was dark and smelled odd. I noticed that her hands were slightly more crippled than I remembered. Her voice sounded huskier than usual, too. Once she started my reading, I mentioned my girlfriend's name to her. Without warning, Iris shoved all of the cards off the table and shouted at me to be quiet! I must have turned white as a ghost because she calmed herself inside of three seconds flat. I looked straight into her eyes and asked her to tell me her real name. She simply began to mutter something about the angels would never win. As if I could fly, I lifted myself out of my chair and headed for the door. I honestly do not remember my feet ever touching the floor. That was the last time I ever saw her.

I have to believe that God was protecting me that night even though I had turned away from Him by going there in the first place. I have thought about that event many times. I am so thankful for having left her apartment safely. When we are young, we do not have enough life experience to see what might have been. I certainly did not. I continued to seek out new psychics. I was just more selective as to how I found them. As for Julie's deck of fifty-two, she gave them to me as a parting gift when she married and moved away. It was several years later before I destroyed them in Christ's name.

I have to laugh when I look back at how mesmerized I was by all of these tools of the trade. At the same time, I am saddened at the thought that I was so materialistic. I cannot imagine placing an object above my faith in God now. You might be interested to know that when I asked various psychics about these props, I was told that many of them feel that they are simply a visual aid. Oh, yes! They feel that their clients need to *see* how they get their information. If you give this some thought, it really does coincide with the truth that so many of us start out by needing to see God before we can believe in Him.

> *Try to help those who argue against you. Be merciful to those who doubt. Save some by snatching them as from the very flames of hell itself. And as for others, help them to find the Lord by being kind to them, but be careful that you yourself aren't pulled along into their sins. Hate every trace of their sin while being merciful to them as sinners. (Jude 1:22,23)*

Dreams & Visions

This area of spiritualism appealed to me long before I ever paid a psychic to do a reading for me. I acknowledged a dream dictionary as a book based on scientific facts. The author of my particular glossary claimed to have performed dream research on individuals who had signed up to act as guinea pigs in her sleep lab. For several years, I referred to her paperback practically on a daily basis. There were mornings when I could not wait to arrive at work because I had inadvertently left my dream book at the office overnight. Some people drank coffee to start their day. I interpreted my latest dream!

I used to confuse the elements of dreaming with those of a vision. Webster's dictionary associated the two as something imagined within the mind. However, the night that I saw the face of my deceased grandmother peering at me from the foot of my bed, there was no way I could ever appreciate that definition again! Thank goodness I had my dream dictionary handy or else I might not have been able to close my eyes in the dark for who knows how long. As I frantically flipped through its pages, searching for information about this type of incident, my heart was fighting to find its natural rhythm. Once I calmed down and checked on what it meant to *see* the departed, everything finally started coming together. To my surprise, this had been a warning about my upcoming marriage.

It was three nights later before I could drop off to sleep without being apprehensive that my grandmother would reappear. She had come slightly closer to me the second night. On her third and final visit, she was just an arm's length away from me. Something in her eyes told me that I would not see her again. By this time, I had come to accept what was happening and took solace in the tender way that my grandmother had looked at me. According to the passage that I had read in my unique dictionary, she was trying to tell me that my pending marriage would start out to be a rough union, but that I would prevail in the end. This was the only *vision* that I would experience for the next few years. Yet, the *dreams* that seemed to carry a message continued almost nightly.

I can remember a magazine that actually contained an insert specifically telling you how to train yourself to dream in order to make pertinent decisions that you were facing. Since I did not have a subscription to this publication, I went from store to store hunting down the monthly issue that contained this material. It was such a hot item on the newsstand that my search was all for not. One day, upon arriving home from work, my husband surprised me with a copy of the magazine that he had found by mere accident. I was ecstatic!

After practicing the techniques for a few weeks, it was amazing how easily solutions came to me as I slept. I got so good at it that I decided to start a little business called *The*

Dream Weaver. I rushed out and rented a post office box and placed an advertisement in a local guide that contained personal ads and miscellaneous topics. The first and last letter I received was from a prison inmate! It was at this time that I realized dream interpretation was definitely not my calling.

What *is* the difference between a dream and a vision? I can only speak for myself when I tell you that a dream is a combination of people or places that I have seen. When I wake from a scrambling of images and oddities, I know that I have been dreaming due to the turmoil that is alive in my subconscious. Nothing makes any sense and I feel that the dream was just that, a dream. In contrast, I do believe in dreams of prophecy or to be more exact... visions.

I am not referring to the incident with my deceased grandmother. Over the years, I came to understand that even though I awoke and saw her staring at me, I was still dreaming. I had a conversation with my mother immediately after that apparition. She reminded me that the mind is a powerful gift from God. Perhaps I had wanted my grandmother to be with us so badly at the wedding that I mentally invoked her image all by myself. As for the coincidence of the dream dictionary predicting the path of my first marriage, I believe that "mind over matter" definitely came into play. I wanted so desperately to receive a sign from my grandmother, as to how she felt about the man I was about to marry, that I read what I wanted to read within the definition.

When I wake and *know* that I am to pray for someone or take caution in something that I have planned to do, I realize that the Holy Spirit is nudging me to honor the will of God.

As he lay awake considering this, he fell into a dream, and saw an angel standing beside him. "Joseph, son of David," the angel said, "don't hesitate to take Mary as your wife!"... (Matthew 1:20)

There was a time when I had become distressed over falling asleep. I was afraid that I would have yet another horrifying dream about my first love, Hal. By way of mutual friends, I was aware that he was married and had a daughter. However, I had not spoken to him in years. This dream began to bother me because I was also married with children. It was frustrating for me when I would awake trembling. Naturally, my husband would ask me what was wrong. In order not to be chastised about dreaming of another man, I would lie and tell him that it was just a nightmare. The truth was that it was more than a scary dream; it was a vision. Hal was in some kind of trouble. For some reason, I was being called upon to help him...... but how?

The dream would always begin with Hal and his wife sitting in a living room engaged in a serious conversation. Subsequently, an argument would ensue. As the sky outside of their home turned eerily black, the walls and windows that were made of glass would begin to shatter! Suddenly, Hal would scream my name and that is when I would wake up dripping with sweat and shaking uncontrollably. After the second night of having this dream, I prayed that I would not have it again so that I could get some sleep. I was not yet aware that it *was* a vision. By the fourth night, I was beginning to understand that I was supposed to help Hal through prayer. I began to pray daily for his safety and peace of mind since I had no idea as to his whereabouts or situation. Still, the vision continued with even greater intensity. After two weeks of losing precious sleep, I told God that, if I was supposed to actually speak to Hal, He would have to arrange it. The next day, as I was stepping off the bus that I rode to work each day, I could not help but notice a courier briskly walking by. It dawned on me that the last time I had seen Hal he had been wearing the same uniform. At the same moment, I felt a warm stir within my heart. I knew exactly what I had to do! Upon arriving at the office, I placed a call to the company where I knew Hal had worked in the past. I inquired as to how I might contact him and the operator gave me his direct number. God sure did know how to get His message across in a hurry! I was so nervous that I had trouble placing my phone receiver on its cradle. I realized that if Hal's marriage was in trouble, the last thing he needed was for a strange woman to be phoning him at the office. So, I recruited Sam to make the call for me. He was an old and dear friend of mine who had known Hal back in the day.

He also had never questioned me about the things that I told him I knew to be true simply by having a dream. Sam had been on the receiving end of more than one vision throughout our friendship. By that afternoon, Sam had called me back and told me that my special ability had been right on target. He had spoken to Hal and informed him about the *dreams* that I had been having. As it turned out, Hal was genuinely happy that Sam had called and he confirmed that my vision was accurate. The two of them had always known about my intuitiveness. Nonetheless, it never ceased to amaze them. I never knew why God was so insistent that I find out exactly what was wrong in Hal's life. On the other hand, I must have completed His will because from that night on I slept like a baby.

I can feel or sense when the Holy Spirit is revealing God's will to me. There are moments when I actually hear his voice. I realize how crazy this sounds, but it is very true. I do not have to search him out. Normally, he awakens me in the middle of the night. I am not always cheerful about hearing from him at this hour, but I accept the will of God whenever it is divulged to me. I am always comforted by the Holy Spirit no matter what the task at hand might be. Some psychics believe that they receive messages from God through archangels. I cannot say much about this concept since there are a few stories in the Bible where angels did call upon God's believers. However, other spiritualists claim to interpret dreams or have visions of their own through the *Higher*

Powers. Yet, there is only *one* true God, is there not?

On a personal note, I could never wrap my mind around the whole notion of having more than one higher power. The fact that the psychics I saw never once mentioned God's name during a reading should have been the largest red flag of all in my mind. In spite of this, I continued to enjoy the nonsense that I was paying for even though I left a number of these sessions with dread on my heart. If you are struggling with the Spirit of Divination and need something to counter his antics, I believe that the following scripture will definitely give him pause.

> *"If there is a prophet among you, or one who claims to foretell the future by dreams, and if his predictions come true but he says, 'Come, let us worship the gods of the other nations,' don't listen to him. For the Lord is testing you to find out whether or not you really love him with all your heart and soul. (Deuteronomy 13:1-3)*

Ouija Board

I have already cited this game in a previous chapter, but I am compelled to give it special attention in this section. This is perhaps the most controversial "toy" on the market today. Some people believe that the two individuals with their fingers on the planchette are responsible for the answers given. The players subconsciously move the message indicator themselves. Others are convinced that ghosts from the beyond have important messages to deliver and that the Quija Board is one means of doing so. I have weighed both sides of the argument and I must tell you that people, who do not believe in the supernatural phenomenon surrounding it, should reconsider their stance on this tool. I played around with different Ouija Boards for years. As a teenager, I accepted them as a simple game. By the time I was in my late twenties, something happened that changed my opinion completely!

I mentioned earlier that I played with a Ouija Board at a sleepover back in the ninth grade. Well, that same night I inquired as to the name of the boy I would marry. When the answer came back in the form of initials, I racked my brain trying to figure out who I knew that had a name to match them. I approached every girl at the party and asked them to help me figure out to whom the letters were referring. No one could solve the mystery. So, I decided to write down the two letters on a piece of paper and sleep with them under my pillow. However, the next morning I continued to draw a blank. Believe it or not, I kept that little piece of paper for several years. I was curious to see if those initials would actually match the name of the man that I would marry one day. They did! I honestly did not look at those initials over the years. Nonetheless, when I became engaged to my first husband, I pulled out the box that I had stored a few of my childhood memories in and took a peek at that little piece of paper that I had written on so very long ago. I could not get over the fact that a silly board game had predicted something that would happen so far into the future.

The next encounter that I had with a Ouija Board really blew me away. It took place while I was living in Houston with Darlene and Charlotte. One Thursday night, the three of us were bored with our typical ritual of watching television while we painted our finger nails in preparation for the upcoming weekend. During the course of discussing what we could do to break the monotony, Charlotte decided to whip out her Ouija Board. Darlene automatically found something to do in her bedroom as she wanted nothing to do with such a heathen activity. Naturally, I plopped right down on the floor across from Charlotte. We took turns asking the board ridiculous questions as we laughed at the very idea that it would tell us anything truthful. We probably had been playing around with it for an hour or so when Charlotte decided to get something to drink from the kitchen. In her absence, I got a strong urge to test the board in a way that I had not done before. I put my hands behind my back and closed my eyes. Then, I asked "Ouija" a question in a very loud and demanding voice. A minute or two later, I heard Charlotte scream. She had started walking back into the room just as the plastic planchette began to move all by itself! Startled does not begin to cover how I felt as I opened my eyes and witnessed the occurrence for myself. For the first time, I really *knew* that there was more to this game than I had ever allowed myself to believe. After that experience, I refused to play with Charlotte's Ouija Board ever again.

It was more than ten years later before I had the desire to play with a Ouija Board again. But, I did! I was in the process of getting my first divorce and my children were at their dad's house for the weekend. I started feeling very lonely and somewhat isolated in my new townhouse. I had no friends to speak of that were living in the immediate area. I had come to the conclusion that I needed to find a way to entertain myself when I was alone. For this reason, I decided that it might be fun to have a Ouija Board around to pass the time. I justified purchasing a new board by telling myself that it was only a game. It may not have been the kind that I would have allowed my children to fool around with, but it would definitely help to fill the empty silence I endured when they were away.

Over the next six months, I covertly messed around with the board that was made of cardboard and paper. Nothing *unusual* had happened and I really began to think of it as a basic distraction from my uninteresting life. One night, I found myself getting frustrated with the answers it was showing in reference to my social life. I recall actually talking to it and letting it know that it was nothing more than a combustible product. Within a few minutes, it began to spell out words that were totally offensive. I became angered by this and inquired as to the name of the spirit with whom I was haggling. The next letters shown to me spelled out a satanic name. I quickly moved away from the Ouija Board and started brainstorming to figure out how to get rid of it without someone else coming across it. The only solution I came up with was to burn it. It made perfect sense to me since it was made of flammable materials.

I immediately set fire to a log that was lying in the fireplace. As the fire began to strengthen, I picked up the Ouija Board and tossed it on top of the flames. I waited a few moments for the heat of the fire to penetrate the board. But for some reason, it was not working. I grabbed the board by its corners and flipped it onto its other side. I patiently watched for it to ignite. Still, nothing happened. At that point, I made a phone call to my friend, Lori. I was hoping that she would have a suggestion as to how I could make this demon tool burn. Unfortunately, she was clueless as well. As we continued our conversation, I glanced over at the fireplace and could not believe what I was seeing. The board was engulfed in flames that were an eerie green color, but it was not burning! As I explained what was happening to Lori, we both felt a chill that was indescribable. We agreed instantly that the board must be destroyed right away. If fire would not burn it, maybe water would destroy its magnetic force. I hung up the phone and ran into the kitchen. I grabbed the biggest pot I owned and filled it to the brim with tap water. As I carried it into the living room, I began to pray earnestly that dowsing the board with water would put an end to this episode. God must have been waiting in the wings for me to ask for His help and forgiveness once more. The instant that the water touched the flames, I heard a tremendous boom! Then, as though an angel was standing beside me, I felt a peace in my heart that I had not felt in months. The Ouija Board began to wilt from the dampness and I fell to my knees as I thanked God for coming to my aid.

You may be considering that I was imagining some of the moments that I have divulged in these stories. Well, you would be wrong. All that I have mentioned above is true. Obviously, the familiar spirit that hung around throughout my adolescence remained with me much longer than I thought *or* new demons were assigned to me over the years. This is the only explanation that I have found for desiring this occult tool over and over again. Since I have walked away from the mystical realm, I still get little quivers when I see a glimpse of any element that has something to do with spiritualism. Yet, I am strengthened by the Spirit of God to dismiss the idea of falling back into the snare of Satan. As to the argument between those who side with automatism and those who believe in spiritualism, I think that a person's viewpoint in this matter depends solely on their religious convictions.

Addiction is not only found in those who drink alcohol or smoke cigarettes. Compulsive behavior comes in many forms. Addicts of any kind are bound by a familiar spirit who has taken advantage of their human condition while it lies in a weakened state. It is possible for the addict to break free of this demon by showing sincere regret to God and being forgiven. Still, it is very disheartening when you think you have overcome a habit that has drug you down in your life only to find out that the craving still exists. Nonetheless, God is always with us and continues to show us His merciful love each time that we fall from grace.

For since he himself has now been through suffering and temptation, He knows what it is like when we suffer and are tempted, and he is wonderfully able to help us. Hebrews 2:18

Which Spirit's Which?

-5-

Some of you may recall the old saying, "If it feels good, do it!" When I was younger, I definitely should have had stationery with this slogan printed on it in big bold letters. Although I personally reigned myself in on more than one occasion, I saw no reason why my friends should not follow this motto to their hearts content. In all honesty, I believed that God wanted me to do whatever made me happy as long as I was not hurting anyone by my words or actions. It never dawned on me that, by sharing my experiences about the psychics I had seen, I was enticing my friends to turn away from God. Nevertheless, that is exactly what I was doing.

The episode in my life that led me to this ingenuous discovery was the loss of my dear friend, Bethany. Nine months prior to her fatal heart attack, I had convinced her to visit a spiritualist about whom I had heard. People whispered that she could tell you things simply by holding a coin that had been in your possession. Terri, another friend of mine, went along as well and had a session with this psychic as soon as Bethany was finished. It was at this time that the spiritualist disclosed something to Terri that she had been fearful of mentioning to Bethany. Bethany was going to die! When I was informed of this, I felt nothing but shear panic. I was haunted for days because I did not know whether I should tell Bethany. Having that kind of power over another human being was excruciating. The fact that I loved her like a sister made it even harder for me. The truth was that I felt responsible for the entire situation.

One night I began to reflect upon the numerous people who had told me to stay away from fortune tellers. They had tried to convince me that it was not just an innocent game I was playing. Had they actually been right? Had I caused Bethany to turn away from God? Was it plausible that she would be standing before Him to be judged in the near future? If so, would she be held accountable for a sin that I had initiated? As tears began to stream down my face, I felt an urge to pray like I had never prayed before. Suddenly, something that I had been taught many years before came alive inside of me. It was the teaching about the Holy Spirit being our Comforter after Jesus died. Taking solace in this, I drifted off to sleep. The next morning, I woke with an unyielding knowledge that I should not tell Bethany that there was a chance that she would not grow old with the rest of us. I was hopeful that God would protect Bethany from whatever evil was meant to take her from me. Should the psychic's prediction come true, I asked God not only to forgive Bethany for her actions, but to also have mercy on me for causing her to sin against Him.

When I was initially told of her death, I immediately went into denial. I just could not allow myself to believe that she and I would never see each other again. After I had calmed down and began to think rationally, I started wondering what her last moments on Earth were like. I placed a phone call to her neighbor, Ben. He was the first person to find her. I questioned him as to whether or not he felt that she had suffered in the end. He described how he had come upon her and then told me something that completely alleviated my fear that God may not have forgiven her. With a trembling voice, Ben began using words to paint a picture of what would be his last memory of Bethany. He said that she was glancing upward with her arms resting across her chest and that the expression on her face was one of complete joy! Upon hearing those last few words, my heart filled with relief. There was no doubt that my prayer for Bethany had been answered. Oddly enough, I did not stop to consider whether or not God had forgiven *me*. I did make a vow to myself that I would not pass on any more stories that pertained to my psychic readings.

My objective in sharing this sorrowful event of my past with you is twofold. I wanted you to hear first hand how we can cause spiritual damage in others by merely trespassing on their private beliefs. Our words can be very

65

powerful no matter how innocently they have been spoken. They can cause confusion or even bitterness in someone who has yet to walk with Christ. Also, you must carry the burden of being responsible for delaying their spiritual growth in the end. If you do not agree with someone's spiritual convictions, allow God to resolve the issues of their faith. After all, He knows their heart far better than you do.

You would think that after coping with the loss of a close friend I would have woken up and lost all interest in psychics. Still, I did not! This is the second reason why I integrated this particular story into this chapter. In order for me to help you understand how I could continue consulting with spiritualists after literally *knowing* that God had heard and answered my prayers for forgiveness, I need to point out the difference between the Spirit of God and the Spirit of Divination.

I will start by clarifying that the Holy Spirit *is* the Spirit of God. How do you recognize Him? According to the Bible, there are three definite ways to know if you have been in His company. Your encounter should help you to grow in your faith, receive encouragement to act as Christ would and to feel comforted through learning more about the Word of God as it was originally written. If these factors are not a part of your encounter, you have most likely been paid a visit by one of the familiar spirits.

But the one who prophecies is helping other's grow in the Lord, encouraging and comforting them. (1Corinthians 14:3)

Who *are* the familiar spirits? They are demons sent out by Satan to coax you away from God. These dark angels do not have actual names like Gabriel and Michael, who were written about in the Bible.

Then the angel said, "I am Gabriel! I stand in the very presence of God. It was he who sent me to you with this good news..." (Luke 1:19)

And

He replied, "Do you know why I have come? I am here to tell you what is written in the 'Book of the Future.' Then, when I leave, I will go again to fight my way back, past the prince of Persia ; and after him, the prince of Greece. Only Michael, the angel who guards your people of Israel, will be there to help me." (Daniel 10:20,21)

Demons are simply noted by whatever they are trying to achieve. The Spirit of Divination is referred to as such because this spirit actually takes possession of a spiritualist who does readings by means of a tool. There is another familiar spirit working in conjunction with him that lures you to a psychic's door. Some Christians refer to this evil guide as the Spirit of Heaviness. He is in charge of those of us who are depressed, lonely or harbor inner pain from our past. He had already made himself comfortable within me through my rebellious state of mind. Can you imagine how much easier his mission became once I began mourning the loss of Bethany? I guess you could say that Satan sends out his horde according to what victory he needs to win. A familiar spirit is only active in the realm of man. It is never sent out from God. The stronger your relationship is with God the harder it becomes for a familiar spirit to get the job done right.

> Yet I am not surprised! Satan can change himself into an angel of light, so it is no wonder his servants can do it too, and seem like godly ministers. (2 Corinthians 11:14,15)

When asked about having any knowledge of the Spirit of Divination, most of the psychics I spoke with never got around to answering my question. They would speak of the Higher Powers, but significant names were not mentioned. This was very true even back when I was having readings done. One time I asked Jackie to clarify who these powers were only to find out that they were whoever I wanted them to be! I found it to be even more troubling when most of the psychics I interviewed felt that the information we get from the Bible is invalid. Since the Bible was written by mortal man, some people feel that it should be revised every now and then to reflect upon current times.

I can understand why some people are confused as to the actual *meaning* of the scriptures. The perfect example would be found in Corinthians. It is here that we can find out what special gifts the Holy Spirit allows someone to have.

He gives a word of special wisdom to some, and of supernatural knowledge to others. He gives the gift of extraordinary faith to some, and to others the power to heal the sick or do other wonderful miracles. To some he gives the ability to prophecy and to others the ability to distinguish between spirits. Some can speak in different kinds of tongues and others are given the ability to interpret what was said. It is the same Holy Spirit who gives all of these wonderful gifts. He decides which gifts each of us should have. (1 Corinthians 12:8-11)

The ability to have supernatural information is certainly one of these. Although there are spiritualists out there that pray before a reading and are convinced that their gifts are from the Spirit of God, there are many more that do not even recognize His spirit. These are the psychics that speak the language of this world; not of God's word. Their prophecy is not related to any of the scripture verses. It bears materialistic messages based on human desire.

Keep in mind, that even though someone may possess special knowledge through the Holy Spirit, it still is not *complete* knowledge.

> *For even our special knowledge and our prophecy are incomplete. (1 Corinthians 13:9)*

Therefore, you can never find out every aspect of your future anyway. I wish I would have identified with this fact during my youth! I spent a lot of money searching for advice and answers that I should have used as my tithe to God. The idea of paying someone for this service brings another question to mind. Why should we pay someone for using a gift from the Holy Spirit?

Think about it. I have already been told by many psychics that they are not to brag about this power that they possess. One or two of these spiritualists admitted to losing certain powers, such as gazing over a crystal ball, due to holding on to information that was meant to be forgotten once it had been made known to their client. It is true that both of these details coincide with the teachings of the Bible. Discernment is definitely required when using knowledge given from the Holy Spirit. But, is it not also true that any gift that we receive from the spirit of God should not be bartered for money?

> *Heal the sick, raise the dead, cure the lepers, and cast out demons. Give as*

freely as you have received! (Matthew 10:8)

Yet, I have known psychics who *performed* in front of an audience only to be compensated by a manager of a night club. Another spiritualist I enjoyed visiting was open to doing readings at parties providing that there were at least ten guests attending. Not all psychics will agree to such activities. Still, I have never known a person of the mystical arena to offer their services for free.

I cannot put into words how wonderful my life has been since I left the Spirit of Divination behind. I have received more blessings from God than I can count. All of those years that I spent fighting to recover from poor choices that I had made due to psychic phenomenon left me hollow inside. Now that my life is consistently filled with the grace of God, I no longer worry about those things that are out of my control. Even the roughest moments are exhilarating as I stand by and allow the Holy Spirit to deal with a situation on my behalf. He has brought me pertinent knowledge that has aided me in helping so many people that I hold close to my heart. The Spirit of Divination did nothing more than alter my thought pattern and cause me to make inappropriate choices. If for any reason you find yourself mulling over the idea of checking out the mystical realm, I would advise you to fight the urge and choose to be a soul survivor.

> *For we are not fighting against people made of flesh and blood, but against persons without bodies—the evil rulers of the unseen world, those mighty satanic beings and great evil princes of darkness who rule this world; and against huge numbers of wicked spirits in the spirit world. (Ephesians 6:12)*

www.ingramcontent.com/pod-product-compliance
Lightning Source LLC
Chambersburg PA
CBHW031416040426
42444CB00005B/594